Best Handwriting
for ages 5-6

We hope that you enjoy working through this book.

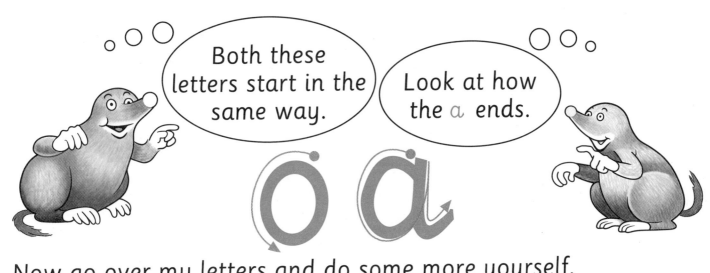

Now go over my letters and do some more yourself.
Take care!

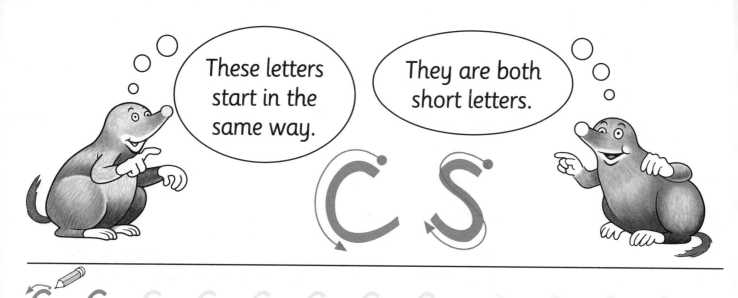

These letters start in the same way.

They are both short letters.

C S

C C C C C C C C C

S S S S S S S S S

Use coloured pencils to complete the pictures.

coat

socks

Letter d is a tall letter.

Look at the end!

Letter g has a tail underneath.

d d d d d d d d d

g g g g g g g g g

Write coloured letters to finish the pictures.

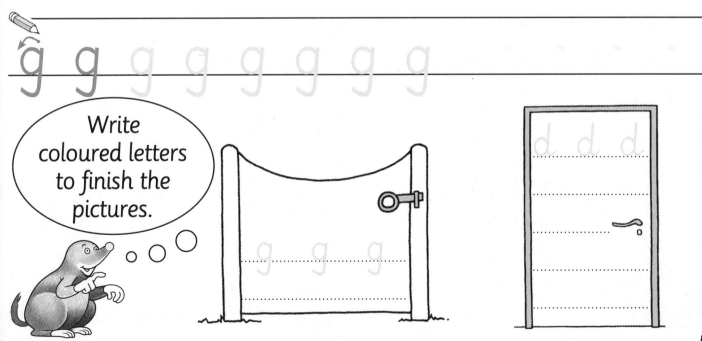

g g g

d d d

5

Letter q and u often go together.

Letter q has a tail under the line.

Look at the end of u.

q q q q q q q q q q q

u u u u u u u u u u u

Put q and u in the squirrel queue.

6

Letters *i* and *e* are short letters.

Look how *i* ends.

Make the letter first then add the dot.

Fill the iron and the eggs with letters.

iron

eggs

7

Make n and m with care.

Look at the end of each letter.

n m

n n n n n n n n n

m m m m m m m m

Complete the pictures and copy the words.

m m m

mouth
m

nose
n

n n n

9

Make letters p and r.

p r

p p p p p p p p

r r r r r r r r

Write the word inside the pram.

pram p

Letters l and k are tall letters.

Fill in the sack and clock.

sack

clock

12

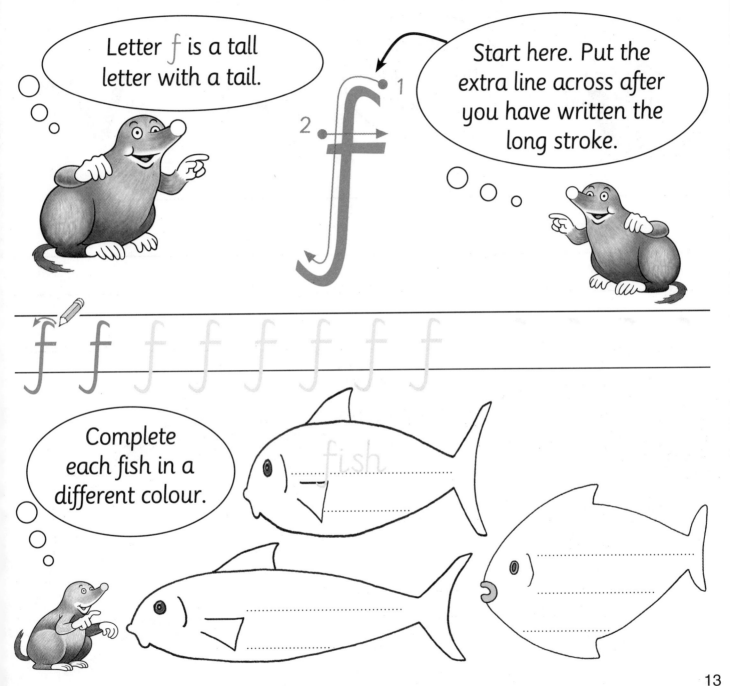

Letter f is a tall letter with a tail.

Start here. Put the extra line across after you have written the long stroke.

Complete each fish in a different colour.

fish

Look at how w and v finish.

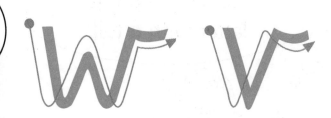

Complete the pictures.

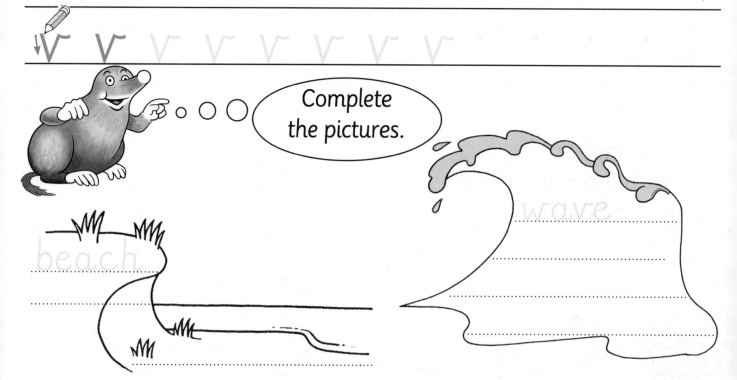

beach

wave

Remember that x and z are short letters.

X X X X X X X X

Z Z Z Z Z Z Z Z

Complete the pictures.

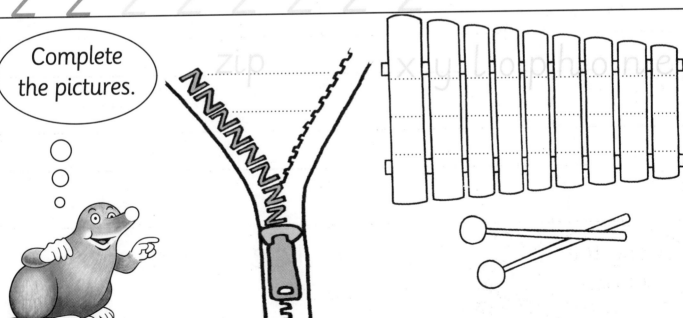

zip

xylophone

15

You should know how to write each capital letter correctly.

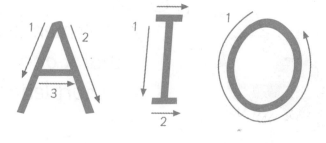

Every sentence must begin with a capital letter. Names begin with capital letters too.

AaAa AaAa

Ii Ii Ii Ii

Oo Oo Oo Oo

Copy the words.

I like ice cream.

Look at these capital letters.

E U X

Ee Ee Ee Ee

Uu Uu Uu Uu

Xx Xx Xx Xx

Copy the writing.

Eat fruit every day.

Write these capital letters carefully.

B C D

B b   B b   B b   B b

C c   C c   C c   C c

D d   D d   D d   D d

Copy the writing and colour my picture.

Big dogs
bark loudly.

Write these capital letters carefully.

F G H

Ff Ff Ff Ff

Gg Gg Gg Gg

Hh Hh Hh Hh

Copy the writing and colour this picture.

Green frogs have four flowers.

19

Write these capital letters with care.

S s S s S s S s

Q q Q q Q q Q q

Copy the writing and colour the picture.

Quacking ducks swim slowly.

Here are the capital letters P, Y and J.

P   Y   J

P p   P p   P p   P p

Y y   Y y   Y y   Y y

J j   J j   J j   J j

Purple parrots love yellow jelly.

L M N

Ll Ll Ll Ll Ll

Mm Mm Mm

Nn Nn Nn Nn

Little mice need long legs.

22

Write these capital letters with care.

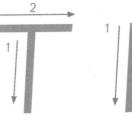 

R r R r R r R r

T t T t T t T t

K k K k K k K k

The king likes red robes.

Write the capital letters V, W and Z

V W Z

Vr Vr Vr Vr

Ww Ww Ww Ww

Zz Zz Zz Zz

A very sleepy walrus was dozing.

The cat and the rat sat in the hat.

_____

_____

Letters f, g and p all hang below the line.

Write coloured letters in the picture.

f g p

The goose and the parrot sat by the fire.

Remember that m and n start at the top.

Complete the picture with coloured letters.

Copy this sentence.

A mouse reading a newspaper.

28

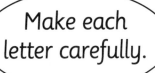

Make each letter carefully.

Leave a space between each word.

The king and

queen wear

golden crowns.

Sam squirrel is smiling.

Copy each letter with care.

Start in the correct place.

a b c d e f g h i j k l m

n o p q r s t u v w x y z

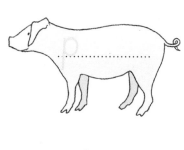

Well done.

Complete the pictures with coloured letters.

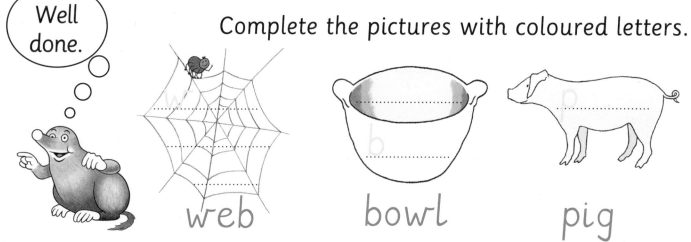

web   bowl   pig

30

Alphabetical Letters

Fill in the missing letters.

You have been given a starting point to help you to make each letter correctly.

a b _c_ d   m _n_ o p   k l _m_ n

_w_ x y z   d _e_ f g   r _s_ t u

b c _d_ e   e _f_ g h   p q _r_ s

i j _k_ l   m n _o_ p   o p _q_ r

Practise your writing.

This is a poem.
Every line must begin
with a capital letter.

1, 2, 3,

_____

Mother caught a flea

_____

Put it in a teapot

_____

And made a cup of tea.

_____